The Art of Mindfulness & Meditation

Overcome Anxiety, Stress & Fatigue Through the Practice of Mindfulness & Meditation

Brooke Henderson

©Copyright 2023 by Cascade Publishing

All rights reserved.

It is not legal to reproduce, duplicate, or transmit any part of this document in either electronic means or in printed format. Recording of this publication is strictly prohibited.

Table of Contents

Chapter 1: An Introduction to Mindfulness and Meditation 1

    The Benefits of Mindfulness and Meditation 4

    The Basics of Mindfulness Meditation 8

Chapter 2: Using Mindfulness and Meditation to Help You Combat Your Struggles 12

    1. Using Mindfulness and Meditation to Combat Anxiety ... 13

    The Most Common Symptoms of Anxiety 14

    2. Using Mindfulness and Meditation to Combat Depression 16

    The Most Common Symptoms of Depression 17

    3. Using Mindfulness and Meditation to Combat Stress 18

    The Most Common Symptoms of Stress 20

    Treating These Issues Using Mindfulness and Meditation 22

Chapter 3: Different Meditation Techniques 27

    The Most Commonly Used Meditation: Mindfulness Meditation 28

    How to Practice Mindfulness Meditation 28

    The Body Scan Meditation 29

    Loving Kindness Meditation 32

How to Find the Right Kind of Meditation for You 34

Chapter 4: Using Mindfulness in Other Areas of Your Life 37

Mindful Eating 37
Mindful Commuting 40
Mindful Observation 43
Mindful Working 44

Chapter 5: Mindfulness Exercises and Meditation Transcripts 48

Breath Awareness 48
Spiritual Meditation 50

Conclusion 53

Chapter 1:
An Introduction to Mindfulness and Meditation

In the world we live in today, many misconceptions exist about meditation. For example, think about what comes to mind when you hear the words "mindfulness and meditation."

You may think of a guru sitting cross-legged on a pashmina and chanting a mantra. You may think of monks as you see them in movies. You may think of middle-aged women sitting in a circle wearing yoga gear and swaying this way and that. All of the above examples are common myths about meditation, which have nothing to do with the reality that is meditation or mindfulness.

You may be surprised to learn that you can practice mindfulness while doing virtually any task. You can practice mindfulness while washing the dishes, while eating, and even while driving! The greatest part about it is that nobody can tell that you are 'meditating' while you are practicing mindfulness.

Mindfulness and meditation come in many different forms, whether it's the act of meditating during a yoga session or a prescribed Cognitive Behavioral Therapy course.

Mindfulness is found as a part of many different exercises and techniques that aim to help people live a happier life.

Before diving into this book, we are going to first learn the basics of mindfulness and meditation.

Mindfulness is the state of mind that is most commonly achieved through the use of meditation. The most accurate definition of mindfulness and meditation has been developed by psychology professionals in recent years. The definition states that *meditation is a way to achieve mindfulness and that mindfulness is a method of focusing one's thoughts and mind on an activity, thought, or object to train their awareness and attention.* The goal of this is to help the individual achieve clear-headedness and an emotionally calm and stable state. You may think that mindfulness sounds easy in theory but it can prove difficult to achieve in practice. Mindfulness requires strong self-discipline and sometimes listening to a single mindfulness podcast or going to one mindfulness class isn't enough to help you become a mindful person. Although, this is a great introduction, a little more dedication is needed.

What exactly does this entail? There is a famous quote by Pema Chodron that helps to illustrate this concept;

"Meditation is a process of lightening up, of trusting the basic goodness of what we have and who we are, and of realizing that any wisdom that exists, exists in what we already have. We can lead our life to become more awake to who we are and what we're doing rather than trying to improve or change or get rid of who we are or what we're doing. The key is to wake up, to become more alert, more inquisitive, and curious about ourselves."

This quote helps describe meditation in its purest form.

Mindfulness and meditation are said to have been developed in the Vedas in 1500 BCE. The Vedas are a collection of ancient religious texts and hymns written in India between 1500 and 1000 BCE.

This could mean that meditation was first developed in India, as you may have suspected. In India, there exists the tradition of *Gurus and Shishyas*, which is the modern-day equivalent of a teacher and their disciple. Students of this tradition were sent to schools that were located in forests to learn and live under a successful teacher. During this time, all of the learning and knowledge on this topic were passed on through word of mouth. In many Hindu religious texts, meditation was written about in some form or another. Due to this fact, we can assume that meditation was an integral part of the knowledge that Gurus were passing down to their disciples - and this was all done through oral tradition. We can all safely assume then, that if most of the early meditation was done by way of word of mouth, we can speculate that the practice of meditation may date back to a time well before 1500 BCE!

You may be saying to yourself, "But how can I devote the time and energy to learn from a guru when I have to work and raise my children?" We will address this here.

In our modern societies, the majority of people are not able to dedicate a lifetime along with the energy that it would take to learn from a Guru, as this would involve moving to a remote area to study mindfulness and meditation.

Due to our evolving society, mindfulness and meditation education has changed drastically throughout the centuries. These days, mindfulness and meditation practices are encouraged as an act that we can perform in our own homes with ease. Meditation is much more easily accessible now, especially since the advent of the internet.

The most popular reason that people decide to learn meditation is actually to achieve mindfulness as a means of helping them combat mental obstacles.

If you are someone that lives a very fast-paced and stressful life, mindfulness and meditation can help you manage your own thoughts and emotions and bring you more peace and clarity.

Many doctors who specialize in the area of mental health have begun to study and even practice meditation and mindfulness techniques with their patients to promote a healthier brain and mindset. Others practice meditation and mindfulness to reach a certain level of spirituality.

Throughout this book, you will learn how to employ mindfulness and meditation techniques in your own life so that you can reap the benefits of this kind of lifestyle!

The Benefits of Mindfulness and Meditation

Now that you know the basics of what mindfulness and meditation are, we are going to spend some time discussing the benefits that the practice of meditation and the state of mindfulness can bring to a person's life.

We will be exploring several of the countless benefits that meditation can offer, such as improved sleep quality, emotional health, compassion, pain management, and addiction management.

As you read through this segment, pay attention to which benefits you deem the most desirable and which you want to achieve in your own life. This will help you decide which methods of mindfulness you want to personally employ.

1. Mindfulness and meditation to reduce your stress levels.

This is the most common ailment that people decide to pick up meditation for. A recent study of 3,500 adults showed that meditation did in fact live up to its reputation for reducing stress. Stress, whether it be mental or physical is caused by the increased levels of *cortisol* which is a stress hormone in our bodies. It is responsible for all the unhealthy symptoms of stress. These symptoms can range from sleep disruption to depression and anxiety, and in some cases, increased blood pressure. It is also a regular contributor to overall fatigue and foggy thinking. Meditation helps battle stress effectively because being mindful is stress' kryptonite. Naturally, when humans are in a state of stress, our minds start to go crazy and run about. We begin thinking of all the worst-case scenarios and how that would lead to our untimely demise.

2. Mindfulness and meditation to improve your emotional health.

Meditation has been proven to help with a person's emotional health and mental health. Similar to how stress and anxiety are partners in crime - emotional health is the overall state of your mind. Lowering negative emotions such as stress and anxiety leaves room in your mind for more positive emotions such as happiness and calmness. There are forms of meditation out there that can help a person lead to a better self-image and build a life in a more positive light. In the same study discussed above, those who meditated experienced long-term decreases in depression and better overall emotional health. A few other scientific studies suggest that meditation can treat depression by decreasing cytokines. Cytokines are inflammatory chemicals in your brain that are released in response to stress which affects a person's mood negatively and can lead to depression in the long run.

3. Mindfulness and meditation to increase your sleep quality.

One of the most noted benefits is that meditation helps improve sleep quality and prevents insomnia. Shockingly, nearly 50% of the population in the world will encounter insomnia in their life at some point. Meditation and mindfulness help you to acknowledge thoughts, and subsequently permit them to pass through your mind allowing you to clear your body of any lingering deliberations. Being able to acknowledge thoughts and let them go plays a huge part in one's ability to fall asleep. If you have many things on your mind, it tends to lead to the inability to fall asleep. It unfortunately promotes stress and anxiety, which is a good night's sleep worst nightmare. One study related two meditation and mindfulness courses by assigning participants at random to one of two groups. The first group participated in meditation while the second group did not. The first group who meditated were able to fall asleep quicker and remained asleep longer in comparison to the second group who did not meditate. Becoming experienced in meditation and mindfulness helps one control and redirect the "runaway" or "leftover" thoughts in one's head which often leads to insomnia. Furthermore, meditation helps you to relax your entire body releasing any built-up tension. It can then place you into a peaceful state of mind where you will be more likely to fall asleep.

4. Mindfulness and meditation to help you become kinder to others, and also yourself.

One of the more known benefits of meditation is that it helps cultivate kindness. Some types of meditation focus more on increasing positive actions and feelings towards others, and of course, yourself. Metta for example, is a type of meditation that is more commonly known as loving-kindness meditation. Its entire theory rests on developing compassionate thoughts and perceptions toward your inner self. With training, people learn to show gentleness and compassion externally - usually to friends, acquaintances, and even "enemies". It is proven to be easier to extend compassion and kindness externally than internally. By mastering kindness externally, it helps one give more compassion and kindness to themselves. In a recent study consisting of 100 adults; they were assigned at random to a loving-kindness meditation practice program. Researchers found that the benefits of this practice were dependent on dosage. Particularly, the more effort and time that the people put into the loving-kindness meditation, the more positive feelings of kindness they experienced. Another similar study proved that the beneficial feelings people develop after practicing loving-kindness meditation can help with anger management, marital conflict, and overall social anxiety. Another conclusion that was drawn in these studies was that these benefits appear to grow over time with the continual practice of this meditation.

5. Mindfulness and meditation to improve your ability to manage pain.

Over the years, research has revealed that meditation can improve a person's pain management. Not a commonly known fact but, pain is caused by your mind and not the physical ailments. Your perception and feelings of pain are directly connected to your mind and can be emphasized in conditions that increase stress. A study that focused on the relationship of pain and mindfulness used an MRI to monitor the activity in the brain while participants suffered a painful stimulus. Two groups participated in this study. The first group had gone through four days of training in meditation while the second group was not provided any training. The patients that experienced the meditation training revealed that the area in the brain which controls pain was highly stimulated. It was also reported that they had a lower sensitivity to pain. Additionally, another study observed the aftermath of regular meditators in over 3000 participants. Its results were that the meditators were associated with lower complaints of intermittent and chronic pain. Moreover, in a study of patients with terminal illnesses, researchers found that meditation and mindfulness helped manage and decrease intense pain near the end of their life. In all of the above scenarios, all participants experienced similar pain stimuli but those who meditated were more skilled in their ability to handle the pain and even claimed that they felt a decreased sensation to pain. Overall, the many studies conducted led to the conclusion that meditation can help individuals manage their perception of pain and that this technique can be used to aid those who experience chronic pain during medical care or physical therapy.

6. Mindfulness and meditation to help manage your addictions.

Recently, studies have uncovered that meditation can help fight addictions. This benefit is one of the more unheard-of, as it helps a very niche market of individuals.

Meditation is, in layman's terms, mental discipline. You can think of it as mental weight lifting. The mental discipline that you build through meditation is proven to help you work away from dependencies by training self-control and retaliating triggers of behaviors that are addictive. Scientific research revealed that meditation can help those not only increase their understanding of the reasons behind their addiction but also help them learn to redirect their attention, increase their will power and self-control, and control their impulses and emotions. One study taught 20 alcoholics meditation and discovered that the volunteers who received the training got better at managing their cravings and the stress that was associated to it. Similar training can help people manage their food cravings. 14 other studies determined that mindfulness meditation aided the volunteers to control their binge eating and emotional eating.

The Basics of Mindfulness Meditation

The most commonly practiced form of meditation is mindfulness meditation. This is also the most general type of meditation to help you facilitate mindfulness in all areas of your life or in the areas that you need. Mindfulness meditation is a type of mental training practice that involves you focusing your mind on your thoughts and sensations in the present moment. This includes your current emotions, physical sensations, and passing thoughts. Mindfulness meditation usually involves breathing practice, mental imagery, awareness of your mind and body, and muscle and body relaxation. It is typically easier for beginners to follow a guided meditation directing them throughout the whole process. It is extremely easy to drift away or fall asleep while performing meditation exercises if nobody is guiding you. Once you become more skilled in mindfulness meditation, you can definitely achieve it without a vocal guide, but this requires stronger mental capabilities and know-how.

In this subchapter, I will be teaching you how to practice mindfulness meditation. The standardized program for this is called the Mindfulness-Based Stress Reduction (MSBR) program. This particular standardized program focuses on your awareness and bringing your attention to the present. This method has been increasingly incorporated into medical settings to treat many health conditions including stress, pain, and insomnia. This method is fairly straight forward; however, it is recommended that a teacher or program help guide you as you start. Most people do it for at least ten minutes a day but even a couple minutes every single day can make a huge difference in your wellbeing. This is the basic technique that will help you get started:

1. Find a quiet place that you feel comfortable in. Ideally, your home or somewhere you feel safe. Sit in a chair or on the floor. Make sure your head and back are straight but are not tense.

2. Try to sort your thoughts and put aside those that are of the past and future. Stick to the thoughts relating to the present moment.

3. Bring your awareness to your breath. Make sure to focus on the feeling and sensation of air moving through your body as you inhale and exhale. Feel the way in which your belly rises and falls. Feel the air enter through your nostrils and leave through your mouth. Make sure to pay attention to the variations in each breath.

4. Watch every thought come and go. Act as if you are watching the clouds, letting them pass by you as you observe each one float away. Whether your thought is a worry, fear, anxiety, or hope - when these thoughts come up don't ignore them or try to suppress them. Simply acknowledge them, remain calm, and anchor yourself with your breathing.

5. You may find yourself getting carried away in your thoughts. If this happens, observe where your mind drifted off to, and without making a judgment, simply return to your breathing. Keep in mind that this happens a lot with beginners, try not to be too hard on yourself when this happens. Always use your breathing as an anchor.

6. As we near the end of the 10-minute session, sit for a minute or two, and become aware of where you physically are. Get up gradually and take in your surroundings.

A common misconception regarding mindfulness is that you NEED to meditate to achieve this state of mind. This is untrue - you don't need to meditate to achieve or to practice mindfulness. There are many alternative ways you can practice mindfulness without sitting down for a meditation session. Let's take a look at some of the other opportunities that exist for you to achieve and practice mindfulness:

- Driving

It is extremely easy for people to become mindless while driving. Especially if you're driving the same route day in and day out. If you're driving to and from work, your mind typically wanders off to what work tasks are needed to be done that day or the chores that you have to come home to once the day is over. Practice your mindfulness in the car as you're driving to keep yourself anchored inside the car. Try to take in what's around you like the color of the car in front of you. The smell of the inside of your car. The way the steering wheel feels in your hands. Pay attention to all the noises you hear, from the music on the car radio to the outside traffic noises. Whenever you find yourself wandering, bring your attention back to where you and your car are in space and time.

- Exercising

Make your fitness routines also an exercise in mindfulness by exercising away from screens and music by focusing on your breathing and where your feet are as you are moving. Sure, watching TV or listening to a podcast will make your run on the treadmill go by more quickly but it won't do anything to quiet your mind. Allow yourself to feel the burn in your muscles, pay attention to how your body is reacting to the work out you are putting it through. Don't just ignore the pain of a muscle, acknowledge it, and let yourself feel the exercise.

- Bedtime

This is usually the time where you run around your home getting everything ready ahead of your next long day which is tomorrow. Don't battle too much with it, you know what needs to be done. Instead, stop trying to rush through it all and simply try to enjoy the experience and routine of the actual motions. Focus on the task at hand and don't think about the next task and the one after that. Leave yourself with enough time to not have to rush through the things you need to do. Again, if any thoughts or anxieties present themselves, simply acknowledge them and let them pass.

- Brushing your teeth

Every single day you have to brush your teeth - this makes the typically boring task of dental hygiene a great opportunity to practice mindfulness. Start by feeling your feet on the tiles, toothbrush in your hand, and the movement of your arm as you brush your teeth back and forth. A helpful tip is to pretend that there is a scanner - and that it is scanning your body from your feet up. Make sure to focus on the body part as the scanner moves from your feet to the top of your head.

Chapter 2:

Using Mindfulness and Meditation to Help You Combat Your Struggles

Every person reading this book has a different reason that brought them here, and each person's reasoning as to why they want to learn how to become mindful will vary slightly. However, the root of everyone's motives are the generally the same; you want to change your life for the better!

If you are unsure of your motive or your "why," take some time to look deep within yourself and address the reasons why you are reading this book or the reasons why you feel it is time to make a change in your life. By taking stock of your true feelings and desires, you will lead yourself to find your motivation for seeking change. Whatever your objective, writing it down will help to solidify it and make it more real. By having it written down on paper, you will have put your reason for doing all of this out into the universe, and it will make you feel accountable. This will keep you motivated when times get tough. You can revisit that paper anytime you need a reminder of why you are taking on such a challenge. Rereading that note will remind you of why it is all worth it.

Understanding the specific reasons as to why YOU want to learn mindfulness and meditation will be the most important part of your journey so far. This is because having a strong reason *why* will keep you motivated, even when the process may become difficult.

Take some time before continuing to find out your reasons for seeking this book in the first place. Are you learning to meditate because you are under a lot of stress? Was meditation recommended by your therapist to help with your anxiety? Do you simply want to do this to find more peace in your day-to-day life?

In this chapter, we are going to examine three of the most common reasons that people pick up meditation and mindfulness. We are then going to look at how meditation and mindfulness can help you to combat these three specific issues.

The three most common reasons why a person seeks a meditation and mindfulness practice are anxiety, depression, and stress. Let's learn a little bit more about these different types of struggles and what they look like before moving onto how meditation and mindfulness will help you to combat them.

1. Using Mindfulness and Meditation to Combat Anxiety

Did you know that anxiety disorders are the most common mental illness in the United States? There are a variety of different anxiety disorders, but most of the time when people use the word *anxiety*, they are referring to the most common type of anxiety, "generalized anxiety disorder." This disorder affects 40 million adults across the world, so you are not alone if this is your reason for reading this book!

Interestingly, humans have experienced anxiety since the beginning of time. Back in those days, anxiety was extremely helpful in protecting us from dangerous situations, such as predators or a lack of food. Anxiety is a basic emotion that all species experience.

The feeling of anxiety is what triggers the fight or flight response, which you may have already heard of. The fight or flight response is the feeling that you get when you must make a quick decision about whether to fight for your life or run for your life.

This is by no means a pleasant feeling or experience, but it is also not always a dangerous one. Anxiety is extremely helpful to most living beings such as animals that hunt for their food or that must flee from predators.

Although in modern-day society, we no longer have the actual need for the fight or flight response, this function is still engrained within our brains and it is near impossible to remove it from our nature. In modern-day societies, anxiety has become a huge problem and instead of helping us survive and thrive, it is negatively affecting many people's lives.

The Most Common Symptoms of Anxiety

If the description of anxiety is something you relate to and think you may struggle with, mindfulness and meditation can help you ease and improve many of its symptoms. Take a look at the most commonly reported symptoms of anxiety:

- Excessive Worrying

Worrying is the most common 'symptom' of anxiety. However, worry is more often seen as the cause of anxiety, which then produces more worry. This results in a vicious cycle of worry and anxiety repeating over and over again.

Worry often occurs in normal daily situations. For an individual to be officially diagnosed with anxiety, worrying has to occur almost every day for a lengthy period of time. Further, the person must have difficulty in controlling their worry which becomes restricting for day-to-day life.

If this sounds like something you experience, you likely suffer from anxiety. Fear not, the rest of this book is going to help you find ways to combat this!

- Restlessness

Another common symptom of anxiety is restlessness. This is primarily dominant in teenagers and children. The feeling of restlessness is often described as having an uncomfortable urge to constantly move the body, or feeling 'on edge'.

This is often showcased in the form of tapping your fingers, jittering a leg, or fidgeting with something. A recent study of children diagnosed with anxiety found that over 70% suffered from restlessness as their main symptom of anxiety. Although restlessness is not a symptom in everybody who experiences anxiety, it is one of the first major symptoms that doctors look for when forming a diagnosis.

- Excessive Agitation

Biologically, when somebody is feeling anxious, their nervous system begins to go into overdrive. This kicks off a series of effects throughout the human body. Symptoms of agitation can include a racing heart, shaky hands, dry mouth, and sweaty palms. When your brain senses danger, it begins to prepare your body to react to the danger, which leads to the symptoms above. This is in preparation for the "fight or flight" response, as we discussed at the beginning of this chapter.

Although this is extremely helpful in the presence of a real threat, it is debilitating in the modern-day, as most of our worries are not physical threats as they once may have been.

- Insomnia

Sleep disturbances such as trouble falling asleep or staying asleep are strongly associated with anxiety disorders. This is likely due to the worrying and thinking that is going on within an anxious person's head.

Similar to some of the symptoms above, it is unclear whether insomnia contributes to anxiety or if anxiety contributes to insomnia. However, it is proven that once an anxiety disorder has been properly treated, insomnia often improves as well. This is due to the strong relationship between anxiety and insomnia.

If this is something that you are suffering from, you are likely happy to learn that treating your anxiety using mindfulness and meditation will also help you to begin sleeping through the night and feeling more rested in the morning!

2. Using Mindfulness and Meditation to Combat Depression

The second cause for many people to seek help in the form of meditation and mindfulness is depression.

Depression is an illness that is often discussed, but do you know what depression is?

A person can feel "depressed" as an emotion, but this does not necessarily mean that they can or should be diagnosed with depression. Firstly, depression is a serious and very common mental illness that negatively affects the way people feel.

Since depression heavily affects how a person feels, it also affects the way they think and how they act. Luckily, depression is a treatable illness and it is something that can be recovered from using the right treatments, such as meditation and mindfulness.

Depression typically causes a person to feel an overbearing sadness and is often found alongside a loss of interest in most activities, especially those that once brought them much joy. It can also lead to a multitude of emotional and physical complications and can hinder a person's ability to live their daily life, including impeding their regular functioning at work or at home.

Why is there an epidemic of depression in recent times? It's almost as if every time we turn a corner, we meet someone who is suffering from depression and/or anxiety. Is the reason for this simply because mental illness is being discussed today more than ever? Or is it because more and more people are being diagnosed with depression?

Mental health experts are focused on researching these questions, but the most important thing at this point is treating your depression. After looking at the most common symptoms of depression, we are going to look at how mindfulness and meditation can help you to deal with it.

The Most Common Symptoms of Depression

Mindfulness and meditation have been proven to help improve the symptoms of depression. If you feel like this is a struggle that you are currently facing, ensuring that you understand the most common symptoms of depression will help you to determine which symptoms you are dealing with and which symptoms you want to rid yourself of.

- Constant Sadness

This symptom is the feeling of sadness that occurs in a depressed person for no apparent reason. This feeling can feel very intense it often feels like nothing can make it go away.

- Suicidal or dark thoughts

These types of thoughts can occur very frequently during a person's depression. These thoughts have to be taken very seriously and when a person is experiencing these emotions, they must ask for help immediately.

- Feeling of worthlessness

A person that is depressed often experiences unrealistic feelings of worthlessness or guilt. Usually, there isn't a specific event that provokes these feelings, they just happen at random.

- Loss of interest or pleasure in activities that were previously enjoyed

A person that is depressed may experience a loss of interest that affects all areas of their life. This can range from not finding pleasure from their previous hobbies to everyday activities that the individual used to love.

- Low energy

People that have depression typically always feel like they are low on energy even if they have not exerted themselves. This type of depressive fatigue is different in the sense that neither sleep nor rest can alleviate this tiredness.

- Impression of restlessness

For some people, depression makes them very jumpy and agitated. They may struggle with sitting still and fiddling with items.

- Aches and pain

Depression can often cause physical pain. This includes joint pain, stomach pain, headaches, back pain, or other pains).

- Psychomotor impairment

Depression can make a person feel as if everything is slowed down. This includes slowed speech, body movement, thinking, speech that is in low volume, long pauses before answering, inflection, or muteness.

3. Using Mindfulness and Meditation to Combat Stress

The third and final reason that brings the majority of people to this book is stress.

What exactly is stress? We have all felt it, experienced it, and dislike it, but have you ever thought about what it is exactly?

The dictionary definition of stress states that stress is; "the body's reaction to any change that requires an adjustment or response. The body reacts to these changes with physical, mental, and emotional responses."

In simple terms, stress is a reaction that we feel when we are faced with situations that are unpleasant or out of the ordinary.

Stress is a normal part of human life and is a natural response, which is why we experience it regularly. Without stress, the human race would not have evolved to the point we have now. Stress is your body's way of warning you from danger or letting you know that you must make a change to your behavior.

The most harmful type of stress is chronic stress. When it is left untreated for an extended amount of time, chronic stress can cause damage to your physical and mental health irreversibly. For instance, poor work environments, long term poverty, unemployment, repeated abuse in any form, a dysfunctional family, or an unhappy marriage can cause a person significant chronic stress.

When a person feels hopeless and does not see any way out, chronic stress can set in and begin affecting their physical and mental health. When a person continuously lives with chronic stress, their emotions, behaviors, and actions can become ingrained and habitual. The wiring of their brain and body begins to change, which makes them more prone to the negative effects of stress on their body.
Chronic stress is a grinding type of stress because it wears people down day after day after day. It negatively impacts the body and mind in a significant way, so much so that it has the power to change a person forever.

Chronic stress can be so dangerous in fact that it can kill people due to suicide, heart attacks, strokes, and even cancer. For this reason, it is important to combat stress sooner rather than later. Throughout the rest of this book, we will be focused on how meditation and mindfulness can help you to change your life and improve your health!

Later on, in this book, we will be exploring numerous treatment methods for stress disorders and related disorders that can be caused by stress. If you think you are someone that is suffering from chronic stress, remember that you are not alone and taking these initial steps will help you to change your life for the better.

Next up in this chapter, we will be looking at the general symptoms of stress. This will help you identify whether or not you feel like you have a stress disorder.

The Most Common Symptoms of Stress

- Acne

One of the most visible ways that stress shows itself in a person is through acne. Scientific studies have confirmed that high levels of stress cause a higher risk of developing acne.

- Headaches

Just like acne, many scientific studies have found a relationship between high levels of stress and headaches. A headache can be characterized by pain that is in the head or neck region.

Stress is the second most common trigger for headaches, which is why it is so important to deal with and improve your levels of stress. By dealing with stress, you can reduce your instances of headaches which will help you to lead a happier and more peaceful life.

- Chronic Pain

People commonly report that they have an increased amount of pains and aches in their bodies when they are under a lot of stress.

Experiencing chronic pain can diminish a person's quality of life, which is why treating stress is so vitally important!

- Frequent Sickness

If you are someone that feels like you are always sick, battling allergies or cases of the sniffles, stress could be the culprit! As you have learned, stress takes a huge toll on people's immune systems, which puts them at a higher risk of infection.

- Insomnia And Decreased Energy

When a person is under high levels of prolonged stress, they can begin to feel that they have decreased levels of energy and chronic fatigue.

Stress affects a person's sleep cycle and could cause further complications like insomnia, which could be the cause of chronic fatigue. A small study found that people who had high levels of stress-related to work also experienced restlessness before bed and increased sleepiness throughout the day.

By dealing with the root cause of your insomnia and stress, it will help you to improve your life as a whole.

- Decreased Libido

Numerous people experience a change in their sex drive when they are going through a stressful time. One scientific study examined women who were experiencing high levels of stress and the effects this had on their sex drive. The results found that their levels of stress were directly associated with their lower levels of sexual interest and sexual activity.

- Digestive Issues

When people are experiencing high levels of stress, they tend to have problems with their digestive system, such as constipation and diarrhea.

Stress tends to affect the digestive systems of people who already have digestive disorders such as inflammatory bowel disease (IBD) or irritable bowel syndrome (IBS) as well.

Living with a digestive issue is never pleasant, so dealing with stress head-on will help you to live happier and healthier!

Treating These Issues Using Mindfulness and Meditation

Now that you understand the most common symptoms of anxiety, depression, and chronic stress and have pinpointed the symptoms that you may be experiencing, we are going to look at how you can implement meditation and mindfulness in your life to combat such symptoms.

As you can see above, many of the symptoms between these mental health disorders are quite similar. If you are experiencing symptoms such as insomnia, it could be the result of one or several mental health issues. Upon reading this chapter, I hope that you have gained a better understanding of the root causes of your potential symptoms. Even if you are unsure, you can begin to deal with your symptoms using meditation and mindfulness, leading to a healthier and happier life overall.

When treating anxiety, depression, or chronic stress using meditation and mindfulness, there are a few steps that you can follow, especially in the instance of an acute anxiety attack or depressive episode. Below, you can view some simple steps that you may take to employ mindfulness in these situations, along with an example of how they can be implemented to manage these situations during and even before they occur.

Mindfulness and meditation are great ways to not only reduce your stress levels but also to get in touch with your body and its sensations. Mindfulness is all about bringing your consciousness to the present moment and focusing on your body, its sensations, the sounds surrounding it, and what it feels like from the inside. Mindfulness involves observing the thoughts that come into your mind and letting them pass by, not paying them too much attention. Mindfulness is a great practice for those who have a difficult time getting out of their heads and tend to overthink more than normal. Mindfulness can be used for a variety of reasons, but here we will focus on its use for reducing stress and anxiety and getting in touch with your body on a physical plane. Mindfulness and meditation go hand in hand. Meditation increases mindfulness while mindfulness improves and deepens meditation. Meditation is a practice while mindfulness is a state of being.

Progressing into a state of mindfulness involves getting quiet and observing, without judgment, everything that occurs within your body. You must let your thoughts drift by, observing but not judging. Pay attention to the sensations in your body; if there is tightness or tension anywhere, the feeling of your chest rising and falling with each breath, the weight of your body on the chair or bed you are sitting on. Notice also your emotions and feelings. By doing this over and over again, you will be able to eventually focus on your body with less and less distracting thoughts. When your thoughts start to distract you, bring your attention back to your body, and your breathing. Being able to reach a state of tranquility allows you to reconnect with your body from the inside and is incredibly beneficial for reducing your anxiety and stress levels.

Approaching your body with a relaxed mindset will also make it easier for you to change your beliefs about your body or introduce new thoughts and behaviors because instead of letting your mind spiral with anxious *what-if* thoughts, you will no longer let them foster and worsen. These thoughts will no longer escalate to the level they previously would because instead of judging yourself and your body and worrying about what is wrong with you, you will approach it as it is and with more clarity.

By focusing on the body and letting your thoughts enter your consciousness one by one, you can untangle them into an orderly fashion, resulting in a reduction in stress levels. The state of meditation also brings about a state of relaxation and calm. Many times, we are running around with a mind full of running thoughts, one after the other or all at once. When we take time to sit in silence, breathe, and sort through everything we are thinking and feeling through a non-judgmental lens, it leads to a state of inner peace. This state of inner peace makes it much easier for your body to process and embrace all thoughts and allows your mind to be more open and receptive.

By trying this exercise several times, it will begin to come easier over time and you will then be able to fall into a state of peace much faster. Once you have reached this level, you can then practice anywhere, anytime with ease.

Now that you know what a state of mindfulness looks and feels like, we will discuss some specific ways that you can reach this state. However, before doing so, remember to be gentle with yourself as you navigate this new and exciting journey.

Some individuals have found that meditation brings about numerous benefits immediately, whereas others have found that it has taken more practice and time to achieve any benefits. Meditation affects you by strengthening your mind and allowing you to be able to control and judge all your thoughts that pass through it. Having a strong mind and awareness is said to help achieve your inner peace. Meditation every day is like a work out for your brain. Think of it as something physical, like looking to gain 10 pounds of muscle in the gym. The first few sessions of your work out might not produce any significant gains straight out of the gates. However, you do feel the positive changes and effects of a workout almost immediately within. The more you work out, the stronger and bigger your muscles grow, and the clearer your mind feels. This is exactly like meditation. The first few times you begin to meditate, you may not notice any drastic changes to your stress levels or anxiety levels. However, you will feel the immediate effects of meditating which is a sense of relaxation, no matter how little or strong that sensation may be. The more persistent you are with meditating, the more you will begin to notice the additional long-term effects. Due to an increase in mindfulness, you may find yourself having the ability to catch yourself when you begin to daydream or become anxious about something. You will start to catch yourself in the act of these bad habits and bring your mind back to the present. In addition to that, because meditation brings your awareness to your present surroundings; you will begin to notice little details in life that you may have overlooked in the past. You may start to notice the intricate details of your house plant, or the shape of the clouds, or even notice new details of your own body. Little things like this in life tend to bring us bubbles of joy throughout the day. Allow yourself to savor these moments as these small joys are what life is about. Throughout your journey of meditation, I hope that you will begin to achieve more tangible benefits such as; stress reduction, increased emotional health, and sleep improvement.

1. **Make a Plan Before any Panic Attacks Happen.**

Regardless of what plan you have made for yourself, having one ready to go is extremely important. Try to think about this plan like a little guide or list that you will follow if you feel a panic attack building up. This may include getting out of the current situation, laying down, heading outside for some fresh air, or even calling your friends to distract you from the ramping anxiety and to help calm you down.

By getting yourself out of that current situation, you can start the next steps in this list:

2. **Employ Breathing Deeply Regularly.**

Since feeling short on breath and oxygen is one of the symptoms of a panic attack, practicing deep breathing could help alleviate it. Having shortness of breath is also one of the main contributors to the feelings of franticness and lack of control. Make sure you are acknowledging that the short breathing is associated with your panic attack and that it is likely not due to a medical condition nor is it permanent.

Next, take a deep breath that lasts at least 4 seconds. Hold it for 1 second, then let it go for another 4 seconds. Repeat the cycle of breathing until you gain control and are breathing steadier. Focus on simply counting to four when you are breathing, which will prevent hyperventilation and will also distract other symptoms from occurring. I understand it is hard to perform in the moment, just try your best and commit to trying.

3. Practice Muscle Relaxation.

If you are in the midst of a panic attack, you will likely feel as though your body control is completely gone. Using relaxation techniques for your muscles will help you regain control to some degree. "Progressive muscle relaxation" is the name for a technique that is great at helping to alleviate symptoms of anxiety and panic disorders.

The first step is to start clenching your fists and holding the clench for 10 seconds. When you reach ten, let go of your clench, relax the hands entirely. Then, repeat this again but with the feet and begin to progressively do this along your body by tightening, then releasing every section of the body. This includes the midsection, glutes, legs, arms, face, neck, and shoulders.

4. Choose a Mantra and Repeat it Regularly.

This technique often sounds a little cheesy or awkward, but it is a great coping technique specific to panic disorders. Telling yourself a mantra while having a panic attack is one good way to center yourself back in the moment. Try repeating simple positive and encouraging phrases like "This is just a temporary feeling." or "I am okay, I will be okay." or "I'm not going to die, I just need to focus on my breathing".

5. Focus on an Object Near you.

This technique begins by picking an object that is in the vicinity of you. Take note of everything you see about this specific object. For example, focus on the color, size, shape, or any patterns that this object may have. Think about where you have seen other objects like this or what other objects look similar to this. You can either think about this silently or you can say it out loud as if you are talking to someone next to you listening in. This technique helps you bring your attention away from the feelings of a panic attack and into your surroundings. By refocusing your attention, you should be able to decrease the severity of the panic attack.

Chapter 3:
Different Meditation Techniques

Mindfulness meditation is the most popularly used style of meditation to solve a plethora of problems some of which we just learned about. However, there are hundreds of other types of meditations out there as well. In this chapter, I will be teaching you about several other commonly used meditations that you can explore as well. These different types of meditation vary in terms of their benefits.

A very important step in your meditation journey is selecting the meditation technique that works the best for you in your current environment. Some of the more complicated meditation techniques aren't feasible for the everyday Joe. These types require proper training from a meditation guru and are not suited for beginners. Most of us will require a more practical meditation technique that allows us to reap the health benefits that we need the most, such as the body scan or mindfulness meditation.

Below, you can find a detailed description of each type of meditation, as well as an example of how to perform it. At the end of this chapter, we are going to look at how to choose the best meditation technique for your lifestyle, so that you can begin to benefit from meditation practice right away!

The Most Commonly Used Meditation: Mindfulness Meditation

The first type of meditation and the most commonly practiced is mindfulness meditation. This type of meditation is a kind of mental training that requires you to focus your mind on your feelings and thoughts in the present. This includes your current emotions, physical sensations, and passing thoughts. Mindfulness meditation usually involves mental imagery, breathing exercises, body and mind awareness, and muscle relaxation. Typically, it is easier for beginners to follow a guided meditation directing them throughout the whole process. It is extremely easy to drift away or fall asleep while in meditation if nobody is guiding you in the right direction. Once you become more skilled in mindfulness meditation, you can perform it without a vocal guide, but this requires stronger mental capabilities than most may have at the beginning.

How to Practice Mindfulness Meditation

Arguably the most famous program for this type of meditation practice is called the "Mindfulness-Based Stress Reduction (MSBR) program." This program was created by one of the students of Thich Nhat Hanh, a highly renowned Buddhist monk.

This particular standardized program focuses on your awareness and bringing your attention to the present. This method has been popularly integrated within medical environments to help treat many health conditions including stress, pain, and insomnia. Most people allow for at least ten minutes a day, but practicing it for just a couple of minutes each day will lead to positive results in your wellbeing. We have run through this one prior together, although for ease of remembering let's run through it again here. This is the basic technique that will help you get started:

1. Find a quiet place that you feel comfortable in. Ideally, your home or somewhere you feel safe. Sit in a chair or on the floor. Make sure your head and back are straight but are not tense.

2. Try to sort your thoughts and put aside those that are of the past and future. Stick to the thoughts relating to the present moment.

3. Bring your awareness to your breath. Make sure to focus on the feeling and sensation of air moving through your body as you inhale and exhale. Feel the way in which your belly rises and falls. Feel the air enter through your nostrils and leave through your mouth. Make sure to pay attention to the variations in each breath.

4. Watch every thought come and go. Act as if you are watching the clouds, letting them pass by you as you observe each one float away. Whether your thought is a worry, fear, anxiety, or hope - when these thoughts come up don't ignore them or try to suppress them. Simply acknowledge them, remain calm, and anchor yourself with your breathing.

5. You may find yourself getting carried away in your thoughts. If this happens, observe where your mind drifted off to, and without making a judgment, simply return to your breathing. Keep in mind that this happens a lot with beginners, try not to be too hard on yourself when this happens. Always use your breathing as an anchor.

6. As we near the end of the 10-minute session, sit for a minute or two, and become aware of where you physically are. Get up gradually and take in your surroundings.

The Body Scan Meditation

The body scan practice is a technique that can be performed multiple times a day to help you identify what you are feeling both physically and mentally. Using this technique, you can learn to release the stress carried throughout your body and mind. When you are stressed, it's very common for the stress to show in different areas of your body in the form of tense shoulders, stomach pains, headaches, etc. During these times of stress, you may be feeling a lot of physical discomforts but won't necessarily connect it to your emotional state. The body scan meditation method is effective in relieving stress not only from the mental aspect but in the physical aspect as well.

Relieving physical tension has been proven to lead to a decrease in psychological stress even when you aren't engaging any external stress relief efforts. Relieving tension in your body can likely lead to overall lower levels of stress which then, as a result, lead to less physical tension. This meditation works to break the vicious cycle of mental and physical tension that can feed on itself. Due to this, the body scan meditation is a very effective and useful meditation technique that can help you stay physically and mentally relaxed. It can help you return to a calm state when you notice that you've become too tense. Here is a basic guide on how to use the body scan meditation technique:

1. Find a comfortable environment where you can sit down and completely relax your body. It's easier if you are lying down but sitting down is also just as effective. Try to find a place and position that is comfortable for you to completely relax but not so comfortable that you could easily fall asleep. Focus your awareness to your breathing. Let your breathing slow down and start to breath from deep within your belly as opposed to up in your chest. Let your abdomen expand, and then contract with each breath taken. If you find your shoulders moving up and down with each breath, bring your attention to your belly and allow the breathing to come from there. Pretend as if it's a balloon inflating and deflating your abdomen every time you take a breath.

2. This is where we begin to perform the actual 'body scan'. Pretend that there is a scanner above you (if you are lying down) or in front of you (if you are sitting down). Imagine that it expels a

laser beam that is horizontal and is slowly scanning your body starting from the top of your head down to your toes. Bring your awareness to where that scanner is and slowly visualize it scanning down your body. Do you notice any tension in any particular areas as you move the scanner down your body? Do you feel any tightness on your shoulders, neck, back, or stomach? Do you feel any sensations of pain, whether it's subtle or sharp? Are you noticing any areas of concentrated energy in your body? If you feel something that is off, try to acknowledge it and think about why that might be the case. If there is tension, release it and move on. Continue to scan your body, from your scalp to your ears, to your cheeks, to your chin, to your neck, to your shoulders and, so forth. This becomes more automatic and much easier with practice to the point that you will be able to do this very quickly and with minimal effort.

3. Make sure you are bringing attention to areas that you've discovered to have uncomfortable sensations. Breathe into them and see what unfolds. Try to imagine the tension exiting your body through the exhale of your breath. A lot of people notice that the feeling of tenseness becomes more intense at first but continuing to meditate through it allows it to dissipate. Keep your awareness focused on that feeling for a few moments, make sure you are staying present. Feel free to give yourself a light massage in that area if it helps and move on to the next body part when you're ready.

4. Continue to do this scan with each area of your body, moving from your head to your toes. Make note of how you feel, and which body parts feel like they are holding stress. Helping release tension in your body now will allow you to be more aware of it in the future so you can release it as you feel those sensations arise.

Loving Kindness Meditation

Loving Kindness Meditation is a type of meditation that helps you to harness your loving energy towards others and yourself. This results in feelings of love and peace that carry over into other areas of your life too. By practicing this type of meditation regularly, you will see an improvement in your relationships and your levels of happiness and life satisfaction.

Loving Kindness Meditation is useful in dealing with social anxiety, marriage conflicts, and anger management. It is also beneficial for enhancing the strength and activation of areas in the brain that are known to be necessary for a person's emotions and feelings of empathy.

Here is a guide on how to practice Loving Kindness Meditation:

1. Set aside a few minutes of quiet time for yourself and sit in a comfortable position. Close your eyes and relax your muscles. Take a few deep breaths in and out.

2. Visualize yourself experience complete physical and emotional wellness along with a sense of inner peace within. Imagine feeling whole and in complete love with yourself, thanking your body and yourself for all that you are and have achieved. Understanding that you are perfect just as you are. Concentrate on this wholesome feeling of tranquility and imagine you are exhaling all of your tension, and inhaling an abundance of love.

3. Start repeating three to four positive phrases or affirmations to yourself. Try to create your own phrases that are unique to you. Here are a few examples you can also use:

    - "I am happy, I am at peace, and I am content."
    - "May I be safe in all my future endeavors."

- "Happiness surrounds me in all that I do."
- "May I be healthy, peaceful, and strong."
- "I am the best version of myself and all that I desire."
- "May I give and receive appreciation today."
- "I welcome an abundance of joy and love into my life."

4. Let yourself bask in the feelings of warmth and self-compassion for a couple of moments. If you find yourself drifting, a gentle redirect of your awareness back to these feelings of affection and kindness. Let these feelings take over your body and mind.

5. At this point, you can decide either to stay with this level of focus for the rest of your meditation or shift towards your loved ones in your life. Start with someone who you are very close with, such as your spouse, child, parent, or best friends. Allow yourself to feel your love and appreciation for them. Stay with that feeling. Begin to repeat the phrases we discussed in step three or create your own that is unique to the person you're focusing on.

6. Once you can hold on to these feelings towards that person, start incorporating other people of importance from your life into your awareness. Imagine them with perfect wellness and inner peace, one by one. Then, begin to branch out to other loved ones; friends, family members, neighbors, and even acquaintances. You can even include groups of people from all over the world. Expand those feelings of loving and kindness to people on the other side of the world and focus on the feeling of compassion and connection. When you are ready, you may even include those whom you conflict with to help reach a place of greater peace and even forgiveness.

7. When you feel that your meditation is complete, you may open your eyes. Remember that all those wonderful feelings you felt, you can always revisit them throughout the day. Begin to internalize how the LKM meditation feels and return to those feelings by breathing deeply and shifting your focus.

How to Find the Right Kind of Meditation for You

Up until this point, we've discussed numerous health benefits of meditation and the most common issues that they help treat. You have also learned about numerous different kinds of meditation techniques. Understanding what you need help with will help you pick the right meditation to use in your own life.

The first step in determining what type of meditation is best for your life is to assess your current needs.

1. Rank Your Needs

Start with what you want to achieve. This can be anything from, lowering anxiety to easing shoulder pain. You can have one goal or you may have multiple goals. However, try to rank them from most important to least important. This way your primary objective is taken care of first.

2. Assess Your Lifestyle

Next, assess what kind of lifestyle you lead right now. Are you living in a fast-paced city? Or a slow-paced and cozy countryside? Or maybe you live somewhere in between the two? Do you have a bunch of responsibilities that take up a lot of your time? Assess how much time you'd be able to put into meditation.

For those who have more free time in their days, set aside a specific time of day, every day of the week to practice it. For those with less time on their hands, think of moments you will have during your busy day to use for meditation. As discussed earlier, this can be during your commute to work, or during the time you're washing your dishes.

Remember this isn't something that will take hours out of your day. Instead, this is merely a few minutes at a convenient time that could result in changing your life for the better. You might find that you actually begin to get more out of your days because of the easing back pain or the settling of headaches that no longer hinder you from getting those extra few tasks done.

3. Match Your Needs

Next, determine what type of meditation method suits you the best. Mindfulness meditation, body scan, loving and kindness, and breath awareness are all accessible and completely viable options to try out.

Mindfulness meditation tends to help people with anxiety issues, whereas the body scan tends to help with releasing stress in the body. On the other hand, loving-kindness meditation tends to focus more on the emotional aspects of a person's life, while breath awareness meditation focuses on managing a person's breathing which is great for stress and anxiety.

Pick one that you resonate with most and that helps with the particular problem you're hoping to solve. The most common form of meditation chosen out of the four is the mindfulness meditation method, as it tends to help with the most ailments and is the easiest for beginners to practice.

4. Assess Your Spirituality

Next, assess your spirituality.

Are you a spiritual person or not? Determining this will help you decide how far and deep you want to take your meditation practices. Of course, this isn't something you need to determine from day one, you can determine that throughout your journey of meditation and adapt to what feels most comfortable to you when the time comes.

A lot of people who are very spiritual from the get-go tend to jump right into deeper-level courses.

There are many modern retreats nowadays in Asia and South East Asia that you can sign up for which will teach you the ways of spirituality within meditation and how they relate to one another.

Coming to a decision on which type of meditation practice suits you the best may be easy for some and hard for others. Don't worry, you can do multiple types of meditation throughout the day and pick the ones that suit you the most to incorporate into your day-to-day life. Remember, meditation does not come naturally to many of us and it's okay to fall off the train. What is important is to not give up and to continue to make an effort to make it an integral part of your day, and life. One of the most difficult parts of meditation is the lack of direction and accountability. Unless you have a Guru at your side who is holding you accountable - it is entirely up to you to keep practicing meditation. Once you get going on your journey, I recommend signing up for meditation or yoga classes regularly to have someone there to hold you accountable. It's amazing what even a few sessions of meditation can do for the mind and body.

Chapter 4: Using Mindfulness in Other Areas of Your Life

Let's discuss how meditation improves your day-to-day mindfulness practice and how it can easily be implemented in your life.

There are many common activities that you do in your life that meditation can improve. These are likely activities that you would not even think of incorporating mindfulness into, but in this chapter, I am going to show you how!

We will be discussing how daily meditation will help you to achieve mindfulness while performing your daily habits. Being more mindful in these areas of your life will bring you a greater level of peace and happiness. Increasing your mindfulness during these activities will also make them more enjoyable and will make them feel less like a chore. Without further ado, let's dive in!

Mindful Eating

The lack of mindful eating is something most of our population suffers from due to the increased pace of our lives. We typically find ourselves eating at work in front of our computer, or eating dinner in front of the

TV, or even eating during the commute to work! This seemingly small issue is one of the leading factors in today's obesity and eating disorder debacle. To combat this, we need to improve our ability to eat mindfully. Mindful eating uses the act of mindfulness to help overcome common eating concerns in our fast-paced lives. The goal here is to shift focus from external thinking while eating, to exploring and enjoying the eating experience itself. This is done to develop a new mindset around food. Here are a couple of points to help yourself identify when are eating mindlessly:

- You are consistently eating until you are overly full or even feel sick.
- You find yourself jamming food down without really tasting it.
- You aren't paying any attention to the foods you are eating and frequently eat in places that surround you with distractions.
- You are rushing through your meals.
- You have trouble remembering what you ate, or even the taste and smell of the last meal you've consumed.

If you find yourself relating to the points above, you may want to actively encourage mindful eating. Practicing mindful eating will enhance your enjoyment of meals, prevent overeating, help with digestion, reduce anxiety surrounding food, and improve your psychological relationship with food. Follow these tips to improve your mindful eating:

1. Start to prioritize your mealtimes. Try to isolate a 15-minute block to sit down and enjoy your meal.

2. Avoid distractions while you are eating. It is impossible to enjoy eating your food when your attention is scattered somewhere else. Try asking yourself how often do you eat while in front of the TV, or in the car, or while in front of the computer? Eating, under those circumstances, is always mindless and can lead to overeating, prioritizing unhealthy options, or not enjoying your meal at all.

3. Avoid being rushed around during meal times. Schedule a time to eat your meal when you don't have any distractions around you. Even eating with a coworker or a friend might not seem like a distraction but due to conversation you might find your thoughts wandering.

4. Always sit down to eat your meal. Try and avoid eating while standing up or walking as these create distractions.

5. Serve your meal on a plate or in a bowl. If possible, serve it on your favorite dish to enjoy the moment just that little bit more. Avoid eating food from the packet or take out containers as it makes eating feel less formal and rushed.

6. Make a conscious effort to chew your food thoroughly. Many people find themselves swallowing too soon and end up with digestion problems. Give your stomach an easier time with digesting by breaking down the food properly before swallowing.

7. Make sure to eat only until you're 80% full. This is a fine line. Don't eat until you are certain you are full but eat until you feel satisfied. A lot of the time the feeling of fullness comes 10 minutes after you finish your meal. If you find yourself feeling full while you are still eating, you probably have overeaten.

8. Take your time to truly savor the taste of your food. Use all five of your senses. Before eating, take a moment to look at your meal and its appearance, smell, and overall appeal. Think about how each ingredient was cooked and seasoned, and how you think the dish would taste because of it. During the meal, identify the taste of all the ingredients. What is the flavor like? How does the flavor change if I eat different combinations of the ingredients?

What can you smell? How does the texture feel in your mouth? These are all great questions to think of.

9. Ask yourself how do you feel about the food that you are consuming. Do you feel happy? Pleasure? Guilt? Regret? Stress? Disappointment? Pay attention to the thoughts that the food brings to your mind. Does it bring up any memories? Fears? Beliefs? How does your body feel after the meal compared to before eating? Do you feel energetic after the meal or do you feel lethargic? Does your stomach feel full or empty?

10. Try to prepare your meals where it is possible. The act of preparing food is proven to be psychologically beneficial and therapeutic. Make sure you are touching, tasting, and smelling the individual ingredients. Take some time with this step as you can really make this a fun and enjoyable time for yourself.

11. Make note of the difference in good, quality food. This tends to be food that is fresh, seasonal, and minimally processed. Fresh and organic foods tend to improve your overall mood and health. Food is our body's nourishment and it provides the nutrition necessary for us to function optimally. Ingesting higher quality food and ingredients is crucial to helping you feel better physically and psychologically.

Practicing meditation is your first step in being able to achieve mindful eating. Allowing yourself to be mindful in your day-to-day life will bring new joys and satisfactions that have always been there but have not been noticed in some time.

Mindful Commuting

We can all agree that one of the most dreaded daily activities is the commute to work. In fact, according to many studies; this is so dreaded that a long commute is one of the major stressors in people's lives that subsequently decreases happiness. The easy answer in this situation would be to just move house closer to work and keep your commute short. However, unless you have tons of money - this may not be feasible for many. So, how do we increase our happiness during the awful chore of the commute? The answer is to practice mindful commuting. By practicing meditation, you will achieve an increased level of mindfulness. Take that one step further and extend that mindfulness not only during meditation time but during your commute as well and reap an abundance of benefits.

Let's use the example of driving to work. This is the perfect place to practice mindfulness. It helps keep the anger and stress at bay when we encounter situations that induce road rage. Rather than finishing your drive stressed out and upset, you can arrive at your destination feeling refreshed, content and ready to work. It's extremely easy to tune things out and get lost in your thoughts while driving. For some reason, our autopilot takes over and before you know it, you have just fast forwarded to the carpark dreading every step taken towards the office. Mindful driving is all about being present during the actual drive. It allows us to move away from obsessive and negative thoughts and gives us a chance to appreciate the world we live in. Here are some tips on how you can practice mindful driving:

1. When you first get into your car, take a few controlled breaths. Acknowledge that you are now in your car and are about to start driving. It is important to leave with enough time to get to work, but also enough time to not feel rushed. As much as we all want to stay in bed for every extra minute possible, this extra time will go a long way to releasing stress. The last thing we want is to be racing down the highway rushing to get to work on time.

2. Turn off your radio and keep your phone on silent. Try to eliminate all potential distractions that could occur in your drive. Check your seat is in good position and your mirrors are aligned.

3. Take a moment to take in your surroundings and the silence in your car. Start to observe the simple features of your vehicle. What color is your dashboard? Do you hear the rumbling of your engine? How does the steering wheel feel in your hands?

4. As you begin to drive, start paying attention to your surroundings. You may begin to notice different things on the route to work that you've never noticed before. Take in the sights, sounds, and scenery of your drive. Admire everything for what it is.

5. Focus your attention on the physical experience of driving. Pay attention to where your hands are placed on the steering well. What does it feel like sitting in your seat? How do the pedals feel against the sole of your shoe?

6. Begin to shift your focus to other physical sensations of in your body. Do you feel the tension in your shoulders or your neck? Do you have a headache? Do your hips feel tight from sitting for long periods? Relax the parts of your body that feel tense and you will start to feel some of the pain and stress leave your body.

7. If you encounter a stressful situation while driving such as being cut off. Try to notice the feelings that this produces. Does it bring on frustration? Anger? Anxiety? Maybe even induce some competitiveness? Acknowledge and identify these emotions and understand why you are feeling them. Often, simply understanding why you feel a negative emotion will help you feel less negative.

8. When you stop at a red light or stop sign, take a moment, and do a quick breathing exercise. Take a few deep and calming breaths 3-4 times before you start accelerating again (obviously

safely and according to the road rules). Remember to take off in a gentle fashion, you are not in a rush.

9. Any time your mind begins to wander, gently pull your awareness back to the present. An untrained mind naturally jumps from topic to topic quickly. Statistically, the average person thinks as many as fifty thousand different thoughts every day. You can't stop it completely, but practicing mindful driving will redirect those monkeying thoughts to focus on the actual act of driving. Remember, when you notice yourself thinking about anything that is not the task at hand - take a deep breath and pull your awareness back.

Overall, meditation, in general, helps with mindfulness in your day. Being able to take it one step further and focusing on mindful observation, eating, and commuting, will help you decrease stress levels and bring more happiness into your day.

Mindful Observation

Achieving mindful observation is incredibly powerful because it helps you become more aware and appreciate the simple elements of your environment more profoundly. There are a lot of beautiful aspects in our life that we tend to overlook just because our mind is used to them. Have you noticed that on vacation you tend to take in and appreciate more of the simple aspects of your surroundings?

By achieving mindful observation, you can find simple joys in life such as; a sunny day, the chirping sounds of birds off in the distance, the smell of freshly cut grass, the feeling of the earth under your bare feet, or the soft fur of your cat. Over time, many people who haven't achieved mindful observation tend to become resentful to the place where they reside. For example; they may only begin to notice the bad parts of the apartment they are living in, instead of noticing the good. In human nature, it is easy for what is good to become your norm which takes away from the beauty of it. Let's try a mindful observation exercise:

1. Choose a natural object within your current environment and focus on just watching it for a couple of minutes. This could be a plant or an insect, or even the clouds or the moon.

2. Don't do anything else except observe the object you are watching. Simply relax and watch it for as long as your concentration will allow you.

3. Look at this object as if you are seeing it for the first time, and remove all racing thoughts.

4. Explore this object visually by focusing on its formation and allow yourself to be consumed by its presence.

5. Allow yourself to connect with its energy and its natural purpose in the world.

Improving your mindful observation is important to help us better cope with difficult thoughts and feelings that cause us stress and anxiety. By cultivating the moment-by-moment awareness in our surroundings, we achieve mindful observation. If we regularly practice mindfulness meditations, we learn to harness the ability to anchor the mind in the present moment instead of being influenced by haunting experiences of the past, and fears of the future. When we master this, we will be able to deal with life's challenges in a clear-minded and calm manner.

Mindful Working

Lastly, let's discuss how mindful working will benefit our everyday life. We have all had the experience of feeling overwhelmed and scattered at work. This could be caused by too many projects, upcoming deadlines, or a sense of demotivation to complete current assignments. Did you know that motivation in the workplace is directly linked to mindfulness? Our ability to stay focused and mindful at work is a way to reprogram our minds to think in a healthier, and less stressful fashion. Below are some benefits to how mindful working can improve your everyday life.

First off, mindfulness in the workplace helps with stress reduction. This is a dominant cause of employee disengagement. The European Agency for Safety and Health at Work conducted a study that produced the statistic that more than half of 550 million working days that are lost every year from absenteeism, are stress-related. Also, 80% of employees report that they feel lingering stress from their workplace and need help learning how to manage it. Some forward-thinking companies nowadays such as Google and Adobe, all have formal mindfulness programs incorporated into the workplace to promote stress reduction in employees. However, if you are already practicing meditation you don't need to worry if your workplace doesn't offer a program like this. You can do it yourself.

Mindfulness in the workplace also leads to higher absorption of new information. Allowing your brain to take a break from developing new skills, critical thinking, and problem-solving helps increase learning and creativity. Not taking enough breaks altogether leads to increased fatigue, stress, and mental blocks. This holds especially true for those who work in jobs that require an extended period of focus.

Adaptability is something that can increase when you are being mindful at work. Being able to adapt quickly and efficiently is crucial at work. Did you know that most employers nowadays value resourcefulness and adaptability over hard skills like coding or programming? Adaptability means that you can quickly adjust accordingly to new situations and handle multiple requests at once. The more you expose yourself to different ways of doing tasks, learning, and gaining confidence in moments of uncertainty, the more adaptable you will become. Adaptability is one of the most important characteristics of excellent leadership performance. It's typically present in leaders who can manage ever-changing priorities and are comfortable in adjusting their perceptions and beliefs.

Problem-solving abilities are enhanced when you are mindfully working. Problem-solving is the ability to remove chaos from the untrained mind. Removing that clutter leads to better concentration which ultimately leads to untying the complicated knot of problem-solving. Also, mindfulness helps with problem-solving by freeing you from distractions and giving you a new angle to attack from. When you are in the heart of a challenge, try to practice mindfulness. You may be surprised at the increased ability to process information in different ways that are required for a resolution.

Being mindful in the workplace also helps facilitate creativity. The fundamental aspect of creativity is divergent thinking. This refers to the ability to come up with ideas that are outside the box. By practicing mindfulness at work, you may be able to enhance creativity which allows you to think more innovatively than those who are mindless. Mindfulness helps free your mind from distractions which in turn boosts your ability to look at things around you from a new perspective.

Vitality in the workplace is also strengthened when you are working mindfully. By definition, vitality means 'exuberant physical strength of mental vigor'. In our case, mindfulness increases a person's vitality, or in other words; their mental vigor. Every single day you go to work with a certain amount of energy. Some days if you've had a healthy sleep, you may have high energy. Some days if you've had a rough night's sleep, you may feel like you're running on an empty gas tank. Sound familiar? Vitality is an essential element in accomplishing tasks while being able to enjoy the work you are doing at the same time. Continuing to stay focused and mindful is proven to have a positive effect on your vitality as it helps you remain aware of your goals and dreams. When your aspirations are clear to you, you are more likely to work towards them with high vitality.

When you are working mindfully in the workplace, you'll likely notice that you have increased empathy towards others. We've all heard the saying "to stand in someone else's shoes". Empathy plays a huge role in understanding the lives of other people, and to relate emotionally with others. Practicing mindfulness at work enables us to free up the space in our brain that is used to feel empathy for other people.

Chapter 5: Mindfulness Exercises and Meditation Transcripts

In this final chapter of this book, I will provide you with some transcripts that you can follow along with, which will help you to practice meditation on your own. These transcripts will help guide you during the early days of your meditation journey and will teach you how to begin meditating on your own one day!

Breath Awareness

The first meditation transcript that we are going to discuss is the Breath Awareness Meditation. This meditation is beneficial in helping combat anxieties and stress that can be caused by our bodies not breathing correctly. Have you ever noticed your breathing patterns fluctuating when you are in a stressful situation? We will learn more about how to combat unhealthy breathing habits that can lead to a decline in physical and psychological health. This type of meditation is thoroughly integrated into yoga culture and tradition. It plays a huge role in every aspect of the practice. This is so important that there are instructors who claim that without breath awareness, yoga is not yoga. The practice of breath awareness did not only derive from the Buddhists but also by early Christian teachers as well. In this section, we will learn the technique of breath awareness in meditation and how it's also implemented in yoga practice.

Breath Awareness in Meditation:

1. Begin by sitting in a comfortable place with your back straight on a chair, bench, or even a cushion. Close your eyes and rest your body for a few moments. Try to soften the sides of your rib cage along with your abdominal wall. This will allow your breath to flow deeper. You will begin to notice a cleansing sensation when you exhale and a feeling of nourishment when you inhale. Be patient, and allow the relaxed movement of your inhale and exhale to become smooth. It will likely take several minutes for you to sense that it is quite effortless. When you have achieved this, you are ready to continue to the next step.

2. Next, relax your body beginning from your head down to your toes. Feel the sensation of relaxation from your toes back to your head. Start to slowly move your attention through the body, releasing tensions just like you would in the body scan technique. When you are finished, return to the top of your head and sense your entire body as a whole. Breathe as if your whole body is taking a breath. Let yourself follow the effortlessness of your breath. As time goes by, continue to observe your breath.

3. Bring your awareness to the touch of the air in the nostrils. Now, begin to transition from breathing with your whole body to breathing with just your nostrils. Allow it to feel natural and comfortable, and give yourself a few minutes to do this. Bring your attention back to your breathing if your mind starts to wander off. Throughout your practice sessions, train yourself to maintain your focus and try not to break your awareness or

breathing. Your mind won't stop thinking so don't expect it to. Instead, just maintain breath awareness.

4. When thoughts arise in your mind, let them come and go. Do not focus your attention and awareness on them but do not turn them into your enemy either. Just simply let them pass by you like a cloud. As you continue through this exercise, your breath awareness will deepen. It will slowly become deeply relaxing and you will begin to notice changes in the state of your awareness. These subtle changes are important checkpoints to your concentration and signal that your breath awareness meditation has nearly completed its inner work.

Spiritual Meditation

This meditation is used for those who want to explore spirituality further. You may not feel any different during this meditation, but you will feel the physical and mental benefits of this practice. During this meditation, you will have to remain awake. This technique can lead to drowsiness. Avoid that sleepiness to experience spiritual effects.

Before we begin this meditation, think about your spirituality. What gives you meaning in life? You will need to come up with a word, or a short phrase that gives you meaning. You will repeat those words during the time it takes to exhale a breath. For example; if nature holds deep and strong meaning for you, you may select phrases that relate to it. Let's get into another transcript.

"Welcome to Spiritual Meditation.

Find a comfortable position for you, one that allows you to remain awake.

Now that you're settled. Let's begin.

Close your eyes. Alternatively, you can choose to focus your gaze on a small focal point. However, try not to get distracted if taking this approach. Start by relaxing your muscles and relieving any tension you may feel in your body.

When you notice thoughts come to your mind, simply acknowledge them and let them pass. Bring your attention back to your body.

Bring your awareness to your breathing. Notice the way each breath feels as you inhale and exhale. Don't try to change your breathing pattern, let it be natural. Just observe.

As thoughts arise in your mind, continue to acknowledge them and then let them go. Return your attention to your breathing.

Breathe slowly, deeply, and naturally.

If you find your thoughts wandering some more, bring your attention back to your breathing.

Notice how your breath flows gently in and out through your body. It feels effortless.

Interruptions are normal. You may find yourself thinking about other thoughts. Let them pass, and focus back on breathing.

Now, begin to think about the meaningful words or phrases you've selected prior. Begin to visualize these words or phrases in your mind as you exhale. If you feel comfortable with it, you can speak your choice of words out loud.

Each time you exhale, repeat the phrase again. Either out loud or in your mind. Either works just fine.

Continue repeating the phrase every time you exhale.

With each breath, allow distracting thoughts to float by your awareness. They do not bother you.

Let any spiritual sensation linger in your body. Don't ignore it, but let it brew deeply inside you. Let it consume your body and let it cultivate and grow.

Repeating your phrase of choice. Feel the spirituality within you intensify. You may leave this meditation at any moment by simply opening your eyes.

Let your body communicate and get comfortable with the feeling of spirituality. Be aware of how it makes you feel.

Begin to bring your awareness back to your breath.

Breathe in. Breathe out.

Let your thoughts turn to your body. Relaxed, peaceful, and calm. Notice how your body feels as it becomes more aware of your surroundings.

Bring your attention back to your thoughts. Bring it back to your regular conscious awareness. You may let the spirituality leave your body.

Stay seated for a few more moments with your eyes open. Enjoy the feeling of reawakening. Savor the relaxation and all the other feelings you've encountered.

Begin to reflect on the experience of spiritual meditation. Be aware of all the feelings during the practice. You should be feeling free from worry and concern.

End this guided meditation by wiggling your toes, and then your fingers. Stretch your back and shoulders. When you are ready, you may stand up and continue with your day."

Conclusion

Now that you are aware of the basics of mindfulness and meditation, we are going to end this book by looking at how you can develop better habits and routines so that you can make mindfulness and meditation a regular practice.

One of the pillars of success in your meditation journey is building healthy habits from the beginning. Building good habits will enable you to incorporate meditation into your day-to-day life with ease. It might require some sacrifice. But remember, your quest to be happier and find more peace in your life starts with you wanting it.

1. Know Why You Want to Meditate

We talked about this briefly in the earlier chapters, but knowing the reasons why you want to meditate is the necessary push needed to get you started with your meditation journey. You need to be very clear with yourself and understand wholeheartedly why you wanted to take this practice up. The stronger your reasons are, the more likely that you can take the plunge into meditation, and be able to keep practicing it.

Being able to recognize, "why" you are jumping into meditation, will give you the motivation you need to pursue it. Having a meaningful reason will remind you of why you started this in the first place. However, not having a reason, or having a bad reason to start meditating is a one-way ticket to an unsuccessful journey, and you may find yourself lacking the discipline to continue.

2. Start Small. Start with Mini-Meditations.

A lot of people tend to be diligent at the beginning with meditation when their motivation is high and fresh. However, people begin to fall off track when external factors start affecting their day-to-day life. Once you stop meditating, or any task for that matter, it's difficult to get yourself back in routine again.

It's not the end of the world if you fall off track. If that happens, take a deep breath, recompose, and start introducing small sessions back into your routine. Set a mental challenge for yourself along the lines of; "As soon as I have finished drinking my coffee, I'm going to close my eyes and meditate for thirty seconds." You will feel accomplished after, no matter how short your meditation was. Remember, thirty seconds is better than nothing. Just do what works for you to get you back into the game.

3. Associate your Meditation to a Trigger

To create a lasting habit, you have to schedule it in to your routine. Even better, associate it with something that you need to do every day. For example, tie your meditation time into drinking coffee, brushing your teeth, or driving to work, as this will help remind you that it is time to begin. Likewise, you will be mentally prepared ahead of time as you know the task is coming up and it will be paired with meditation during this allocated period.

4. Choose your Meditation Method

Being able to choose your meditation method ahead of time is important. You've learned a few different meditation methods earlier in this book, but I will list a few more that you can choose from.

- Take 100 breaths and count every single one. Try not to think of anything else except counting to 100 breaths.

- Follow along with a guided meditation. I have provided you with a few transcripts in this book to get you started. However, you may prefer an audiobook or even a YouTube video.
- Try the visualization method. Close your eyes and begin to imagine that there is a door in front of you. When you open the door, it leads to a beautiful garden. What do you see in this garden? Is it filled with beautiful trees? Is there a pond in the garden? What do you hear around you? Are there birds chirping and bees buzzing? Can you hear the sound of the breeze ruffling the trees? Try to create the most beautiful and peaceful garden that you can, in your mind, and try to stay there throughout your meditation.
- Try meditation apps on your phone. There are numerous apps that help you find peace and tranquility.
- Learn a meditation mantra.

Luckily, there are many meditation methods to pick from. You may try as many as you like until you find one that resonates with you the most. Feel free to change your method if you find that it's not working for you anymore, you desire something different, or if it's not quite achieving the goals you've set for yourself.

5. Make Meditation Fun!

Let's be real with ourselves, how many times have we tried to stick to something that bores us? It's just a matter of time before we stop doing it, and all that hard work crumbles to the ground. A good technique to counter this is to try to make your meditation sessions as much fun as possible. I will give you a variety of strategies and tips to make your sessions more fun and ceremonial.

- Light a candle with a scent that you love. Your brain will associate your favorite scent with meditation and make the whole session more enjoyable and calming.

- Get some incense. If you've ever visited a Buddhist temple before, you may find that there are always a lot of incenses. This may make your session feel more "official" as if you were meditating at an actual temple.
- Turn on some nature sounds or meditation music. These calming and soothing soundscapes will help ground you and make the experience more enjoyable. It's no fun to hear the constant sound of traffic around you when meditating.
- In many Buddhist practices, they use singing bowls to signal the beginning and end periods of silent meditation. You can get yourself one of these bowls and strike it at the beginning and end of your meditation sessions. Just like the incense, it does make your session feel more official.

In conclusion, mindfulness and meditation are powerful tools that can help us to lead happier and healthier lives. By taking the time to emphasize the present and quiet the mind, we can reduce stress, improve our ability to focus, and increase our overall sense of well-being. The techniques and practices outlined in this book are just a starting point, and there is a plethora of resources available for those who wish to continue their journey of self-discovery and self-improvement. Remember, it is crucial to be patient and kind to yourself as you begin to integrate mindfulness and meditation into your daily routine. Nothing changes until you do. I wish you the best of luck.

"The body benefits from movement, and the mind benefits from stillness."
— *Sakyong Mipham*

www.ingramcontent.com/pod-product-compliance
Lightning Source LLC
Chambersburg PA
CBHW041310110526
44590CB00028B/4315